# Thoughts of Idle Hours

You are holding a reproduction of an original work that is in the public domain in the United States of America, and possibly other countries.You may freely copy and distribute this work as no entity (individual or corporate) has a copyright on the body of the work.This book may contain prior copyright references, and library stamps (as most of these works were scanned from library copies).These have been scanned and retained as part of the historical artifact.

This book may have occasional imperfections such as missing or blurred pages, poor pictures, errant marks, etc. that were either part of the original artifact, or were introduced by the scanning process. We believe this work is culturally important, and despite the imperfections, have elected to bring it back into print as part of our continuing commitment to the preservation of printed works worldwide. We appreciate your understanding of the imperfections in the preservation process, and hope you enjoy this valuable book.

# THOUGHTS OF IDLE HOURS.

# THOUGHTS OF

# IDLE HOURS

BY
MYRA VIOLA WILDS
**BLIND VERSE WRITER**

ILLUSTRATIONS BY
LORENZO HARRIS, Artist
PHILADELPHIA, PA.

NASHVILLE, TENN.,
NATIONAL BAPTIST PUBLISHING BOARD
1915

"COPYRIGHT"
BY MYRA VIOLA WILDS
1915

## DEDICATION.

To him of all on earth, most faithful, "My Husband," I affectionately dedicate' this little volume.

# PREFACE.

Total Blind and Limited Education.

I send out my first little book, "Thoughts of Idle Hours," trusting it may find kind, considerate friends. Should I live to finish the second edition, I hope it will be a great improvement over this my first. I was born at Mount Ollie, Ky., a little country place. I lost my eyesight from overwork and eye strain at my occupation, dressmaking, in the year 1911. For three years afterwards, I went through a very severe illness. On March 10th, 1914, at 3 a. m. I awoke out of a sound sleep and wrote my first poem, "Sunshine." In eleven months and seventeen days afterwards, I had written the contents of this book. The question has often been asked, who writes your thoughts for you, since you are blind? I will answer here. Every line and verse in this little volume has been composed and written with my own hand notwithstanding the loss of my eyesight.

A copy of each verse I retain in my own handwriting, after this, they are copied in a book by my husband. I beg your kind consideration of the plain, simple verses herein:

I do not seek Wealth, Fame or Place,
Among the great ones of my race,
But, I would pen in letters bold!
Some thoughts! perhaps to cheer the soul.

*Myra Viola Wilds*

# CONTENTS.

Title .... .. ............................................3
Dedication . ` . ............. ·............................5
Preface .. ` . . ............................................6

## POEMS.

Sunshine .. .. .. ·. ....................................9
A Thanksgiving Prayer ............................. 10
The Early Morning ` .............. ·. .................. 11
Dewdrops ... . ......................................12
My Thoughts .... ....................................13
To Hon. Edward James Cattell ....................14
Little Yellow Baby ........................· ........... 15
A · Sonnet .. ....................................... 18
A Lullaby ...... ...........................·......... 19
Elsie ...... . ......................................·.. 20
The Little· German ·Band ........................ ·... 21
The Best Family ...................... · ..............22
The Babe · That's Dark as Night ...................23
Nature ... ... . ................ ·.......................24
Superstitious ·Sam on the· War ......................25
The Hoop Skirt ..........................·........... 26
A · Racoon Chase .... ................................29
Basket ·Meeting· Day .................·..............30
The ·Organ ·Master ................................37
Bessie . . . .............................................39
A Yoke of Oppression ........................ ·. ....40
Jack and ·I · . ` . ...............................·........41
The · Ladies' Sewing Bee ........ ·. .................42

Thoughts
When You Feel a Little Blue
The Chorus
Ezikiel's First Degree
He Didn't Stop to Think
The Girl Who Does Not Care
Our Exposition
The Old-time Religion
Deacon Jones
A Foolish Man
Spring
Looking Back
Down in the Country
The Wandering Sheep
A Man of the Heart
As You Go From Home Today
He Is Risen
To J. J. Pearce
New Style Tunes
Uncle Joshua's Birthday Dinner
Pity
As I Pass by the Way
Toiling
War in Europe
O! Mighty Sea
Thoughts of Man
The Beautiful World
Climbing Up
Stop and Think
Waiting in the Shadow

# Thoughts of Idle Hours.

## "SUNSHINE."

To C. Garfield Fox, of "The Philadelphia Record."

Like the sunshine, in the morning,
    As it falls upon the field,
Let our hearts be bright and happy,
    And to sorrow never yield.

Let all sadness turn to gladness,
    And our path will brighter be;
He who loves us is above us,
    And our way can plainly see.

Thoughts of Idle Hours

# "A THANKSGIVING PRAYER."

Our land has been fruitful,
   Thou hath given us food,
Clothing and shelter,
   And blessed us with good.

We have sown and gathered
   The ripe golden grain;
Thou hath sent us the sunshine,
   The clouds and the rain.

We've gathered in store
   The gifts from Thy hand;
There is peace and plenty,
   Throughout our broad land.

From the homes of the brave,
   In the land of the free,
We bow, Blessed Father,
   In Thanksgiving to Thee.

For mercy, O Lord,
   We humbly beseech Thee;
For the nations at war,
   In the lands across the sea.

Restore to us, Father,
   Thy love, and thy peace,
Oh Thou, King of all kings!
   Cause this cruel war to cease.

## Thoughts of Idle Hours

## "THE EARLY MORNING."

In the early mist of morning,
As the day is slowly dawning,
Hear the rustling of the leaves
In the gentle summer breeze.

See the flowers lift their heads,
From their peaceful little beds,
Smiling sweetly, bright and gay,
Cheering thousands by their stay.

See the pansy's big bright eyes,
Peep at you in sweet surprise;
And the violet dipped in dew,
Says she has a kiss for you.

The pink rose turned a crimson red,
At the words the violet said;
The lily stood so pure and white,
Blushing sweet, then took her flight.

All day long the gentle breeze,
Scampered with the flowers and trees,
Till the sun which shown so bright,
Left for home and said good night.

Thoughts of Idle Hours.

"DEWDROPS."

To I. Underhill.

Watch the dewdrops in the morning,
  Shake their little diamond heads,
Sparkling, flashing, ever moving,
  From their silent little beds.

See the grass! Each blade is brightened,
  Roots are strengthened by their stay;
Like the dewdrops, let us scatter
  Gems of love along the way.

THOUGHTS OF IDLE HOURS.

# MY THOUGHTS.

Many thoughts had I!
And away they would fly,
From the east to the west,
Seeking some place to rest.

Through the woodland and trees,
'n the soft summer breeze,
By the silvery stream,
For awhile they would dream.

Like a flash of the eye,
Off again they would fly;
As a bird seeks a nest,
For its young ones to rest.

In a garden they flew,
Where the sweet violets grew,
And sought for a kiss,
From her lips sweet with dew.

Then onward they went,
With love in the heart,
And stopped for a rest,
In the galleries of art.

The artist could see,
Love had set them at rest;
And he painted for me
The one I loved best.

## THOUGHTS OF IDLE HOURS

May my thoughts never roam,
From the place where I met
The dearest of all,
One sweet violet.

---

To Hon. Edward James Cattell, Statistician of the City of Philadelphia, Pa.

A master mind was his,
 In the art of calculation;
So swift. his thoughts were wont to fly
 Throughout the whole creation.

The city had appointed him
 To note her great progression;
And keep a tab on everything
 She had in her possession.

He could tell about the city,
 From the first day of its birth;
Her many parks and buildings,
 And every cent she's worth.

His friends would gladly gather 'round,
 To hear his late review,
About the city and its needs,
 And what they hoped to do.

Beloved by all the friends he knew,
 And to his duty stood quite true;
On him the city could rely
 To raise her standard bright and high.

## Thoughts of Idle Hours

## "LITTLE YELLOW BABY."

(This poem was composed and written June 8, 1914, and made its first appearance in the Philadelphia Record, July 13th, 1914. Since then a new verse has been added and the top line changed.)

Little yellow baby,
  With dimpled hands and face,
Where'd you get that dirt from?
  You're surely a disgrace.
Look at those sticky fingers
  My suger bowl, I know,
Old Shivery Slinkum
  Will catch you sure.

Don't grab me by the apron;
  I saw him peeping then.
And when the door is open,
  He's going to walk right in.
Don't let old "Slinkum" get you.
  Well then you best be good,
Or else I'll let him take you
  And chop you up for wood.

Dinah, bring the basin;
  Wash his face and hands.
Don't you dare to whimper;
  Sit up! Goodness lands!

Dinah, bring the basin;
  Wash his face and hands.
Hush! don't dare to whimper

## THOUGHTS OF IDLE HOURS.

Eyes a little drowsy—
  Looking kind o' weak;
Little yellow baby,
  I'll rock you off to sleep.

Whimpering little baby,
  Hush! Now do not weep!
Tender eyes shall guard thee,
  While you are asleep.

Pleasant dreams attend thee!
  Angels near thee keep,
Little yellow baby,
  Sleep! Sleep! Sleep!

## "A SONNET."

I've tried in vain to write a sonnet,
My mind was on a brand new bonnet;
I could not write a line.
Thoughts would come and then they'd go,
I found the task no better so,
I stopped it for a time.
At last I took my pen again,
And tried to make that sonnet plain,
And off my thoughts went flying;
My mind you see was all upset,
About that pretty bonnet.
My thoughts would fly, no use to try,
I could not write a sonnet.

Thoughts of Idle Hours

# A LULLABY—"LITTLE CURLY HEAD."

Come, little curly head,
Bright eye'd baby boy;
  Mammy's gwine to rock you to sleep.
Close dem eyes now,
Mammy's little love and joy,
  Hush, now! Go to sleep.

Mammy's gwine to buy you
A brand new rocking horse,
  And a pretty kite and string,
A little jumping jack,
And a pretty pussy cat.
  And a mocking bird that sings.

Mammy don't care
If your little face is black;
It's just the sweetest face I know.
Dem pearly teeth so white,
And sparkling eyes so bright
  They follow wherever I go.

Off to sleepy land!
Is Mammy's little man.
  Dreaming of his games and toys.
The pretty kite and string,
And other little things,
  And the many fights he'll have among the boys.

THOUGHTS OF IDLE HOURS.


## "ELSIE."

She was fair,
With golden brown hair,
As the autumn leaves,
In an October breeze,
From a child of three,
She was happy and free,
As a lark on the wing,
In the young budding spring,
As the years rolled by,
On her I'd rely.

But alas! one day,
Carl took her away,
To be at his side,
His wife and his bride;
He a youth of good taste,
With manner and grace of a prince;
He was grand,
Just the right sort of man,
For Elsie, my friend,
I trust to the end.

# THE LITTLE GERMAN BAND.

I had stopped down at the corner
　To hear the little German band,
Playing "Away Down South in Dixie"
　And "A March Through Georgia Land."

When I spied my mother coming,
　With a broad strap in her hand,
O! I never stopped to look back
　At that little German band.

Home I went a-running,
　Just as fast as I could go;
In a closet hid myself,
　My heart was full of woe.

When mother found me, there at last,
　There was no use to cry;
I climbed up to the transom door,
　And tried my best to fly.

She hauled me down, with might and main,
　And then I tried to run;
I'll never watch a German band,
　For strapping ain't no fun.

Thoughts of Idle Hours

## "THE BEST FAMILY."

The best family I knew,
Now honest and true,
Was a family of ten,
Both women and men.

It's seldom you pick
A family who stick
So closely together,
As the family of Kix.

The father and mother,
Were faithful and true;
And their children were reared
With the rod that was due.

An honor were they,
Each boy and girl;
And the kindest of friends,
That I had in the world.

THOUGHTS OF IDLE HOURS

## "THE BABE THAT'S DARK AS NIGHT."

They've sung about the yellow babe,
The brown one and the white,
But the little babe I love the best
Is the one that's dark as night.

You see he has such sparkling eyes,
Bright as they can be;
He looks so cute and cunning-like,
When'er he smiles at me.

He's just the funniest little scamp
You'd find for miles around;
I love to jump him on my knee,
And trot him off to town.

"Dot Tanny now?" he said to me,
His little heart was full of glee;
When from my pocket wide and deep,
I pulled him out a candy sheep.

'Twas fun to see his big bright eyes,
Beam out with joy and glad surprise,
He laughed and jumped and ran and peeped,
Until he almost fell asleep.

It filled my heart with great delight,
To see that babe as dark as night,
A-sleeping sweet in slumber deep,
Still holding tight his candy sheep.

# Thoughts of Idle Hours.

## "NATURE."

Nature in the earth has slumbered,
   Through the chilly winter's blasts;
Beasts have sought their caves for shelter,
   Till the ice and snow have past.

Birds have sought a land of sunshine,
   Through the southern fields they roam;
Making merry with their singing,
   Winter o'er, they come back home.

Spring is near, the streams are swelling,
   Nature, too, is on her way;
Birds and beasts are fast returning,
   All the world seems bright and gay.

Thoughts of Idle Hours.

# "SUPERSTITIOUS SAM ON THE WAR."

Things are getting mighty tangled,
    In de world des latter days;
And dey sends your thoughts a-flying,
    In a thousand different ways.

Well, de world is just as bright,
    As it's always been to me;
But dar's something wrong, my brud'r,
    Just as wrong as wrong can be.

Dah's de nations of de earth,
    Dey ain't satisfied to stay;
In de worl' so full and fruitful,
    Where dey haves it all de'r way.

Now, dah ain't no use in talkin',
    Somp'em will hap'en shoe's you born;
If de folks don't stop dare fighting,
    Gable shore will blow de horn.

Den dar'l be no use in stop'in',
    Fur dey won't have time to pray;
Fur when Gable blows that mighty horn,
    Dar'l be de judgment day.

## Thoughts of Idle Hours

## "THE HOOP SKIRT."

You can talk about the new style gowns,
   And high-heeled boots they wear,
The puffs and curls and other things,
   That fashion now call hair.

But you ought to seen my mother,
   In her hoop skirts, bless her soul;
With her waterfall of cotton,
   Dyed black as furnace coal.

I remember standing by her,
   In those good old-fashioned days;
While her hoop skirt bobbed and noddled,
   In a dozen different ways.

Thinking how she'd ever stop them,
   When she sat her down to spin,
While a-standing there a-thinking,
   Deacon Jones come walking in.

Good morning, Sister Mandy!
   Said the deacon with a bow;
Is John at home? I come to see
   If he'll go and help me plow.

## Thoughts of Idle Hours

I am sorry, said my mother,
　John has gone in town today,
With some chickens, eggs and butter,
　And a load of new mown hay.

Have a chair, my mother offered;
　Now when John comes back from town
I'll remember 'bout the plowing,
　And will sure to send him round.

Thank you, said the deacon,
　Well, I guess I'll have to go;
Mother's hoop skirt bobbed and noddled,
　As she stood there in the door.

Give my love to Sister Sally,
　Mother called out with a smile;
Tell her Sunday is baptizing,
　Up the road here 'bout a mile.

Brother Jasper will preach the sermon,
　In the morning, and at night
We will have another brother
　By the name of Isaiah White.

Then she sat down to her spinning,
　In her usual pleasant way,
Singing sweetly, "Roll on, Jordan,
　Till that bright and happy day."

## Thoughts of Idle Hours

After all I think that fashion,
  With its funny styles and ways,
Will welcome back the hoop skirt,
  Of those good old-fashioned days.

## Thoughts of Idle Hours

# "A Racoon Chase."

Ike and me, just him and me,
Went on a racoon chase.
Over hill and dale we found the trail,
But lost it in our haste.

Said Ike to me, that coon you see,
I think went up that 'simmon tree;
Said I to Ike, well, I'll be bound,
I'll climb that tree and fetch him down.

Oh, no! said Ike, just let him be,
That coon is wise as you and me;
We saw his shadow on the ground,
That scamp was slowly sneaking down.

I called to Ike to bring the dogs,
I'd chase that coon behind some logs;
He called old Roscow, Nero, too.
That coon got out and fairly flew.

As far as me and Ike could see,
That scamp ran up another tree;
The dogs, they ran and jumped and bound,
And tried their best to bring him down.

I looked at Ike,
Ike said to me,
That coon can have that 'simmon tree.

Thoughts of Idle Hours

## "BASKET MEETING DAY."

(This scene was taken from a little place in the hills of Kentucky called Mount Ollie, not far from my birthplace.)

Time was drawing mighty near,
  To basket meeting day,
Down at Mt. Ollie where they say
  The yearly spread is laid.

Every buggy in the town,
  Wagon, cart and dray,
Had been engaged for weeks ahead
  For basket meeting day.

Sis Hannah Brown, who always led
  In everything that's great,
Sent word to all her friends around,
  To start in and not wait.

There's cakes to bake and pies to make,
  Peach preserves and jam,
Biscuits brown and hoe cakes too,
  Perhaps a dozen hams.

The chickens, when it comes to them,
  They took the cue and flew;
For miles around no fowl was found,
  What would the preacher do?

# THOUGHTS OF IDLE HOURS

The chickens when it came to them,
  They took the cue and flew;
For miles around, no fowl was found,
  What would the preacher do?

## Thoughts of Idle Hours.

The great eventful day arrived,
   They came from miles around,
From Johnson's place and Thompson's place,
   And lots of folks from town.

The day had started bright and fair,
   As anyone could wish;
The deacons they were on the grounds,
   To help on with the rush.

By twelve o'clock the yard was full,
   No room for man or beast;
The church was full and wagons full,
   Where would they spread the feast?

The meeting house was quite too small,
   To hold the surging crowd;
And Parson Sparks had had his pulpit
   Moved out in the yard.

He mounted high and took his stand,
   And then began to speak;
My text said he shall be this day
   "The shepherd and the sheep."

I have prepared on my right hand,
   A pasture for the sheep,
And on my left a stopping place,
   Where sinners come to weep.

He mounted high and took his stand,
And then began to speak;
"My text," said he, "shall be this day,
'The Shepherd and the sheep.'"

## Thoughts of Idle Hours

Come right on up and take your place,
  The parson gave command;
And all at once the surging crowd
  Had marched on his right hand.

"Praise the Lamb!" a brother cried;
  And then the shouting started;
High in the air flew hats and hair,
  For heads and hair had parted.

They shouted in and shouted out,
  Till almost time for dinner;
The parson cried, "Now friends, sit down,"
  I cannot find a sinner."

Take your seats," he said again;
  And with his hand he waved.
"I find no goats are here today,
  There is nothing but the saved.

"Brother Pierce, please come up front,
  And take the day's collection;
Now, friends, each one must do his best,
  That it may bear inspection.

"Deacon Dodd, please start a hymn,
  With plenty money in it;

Praise the Lamb! a brother cried;
And then the shouting started

## Thoughts of Idle Hours

(Hymn.)

I been listening all night long,
  I been listening all day;
I been listening all night long,
  To hear some sinner pray.

"Come right on up, don't sit and wait,
  It's almost time for eating;
At any rate it's growing late."
  Thus ends our basket meeting.

THOUGHTS OF IDLE HOURS.

## "THE ORGAN MASTER."

(To Mr. John A. Lively, Philadelphia, Pa., February 9th, 1915.)

We've got a great big organ
    At the church down where I go;
And you ought to hear the music,
    Playing softly, sweet and low.

They've as fine an organ master
    As is found in any town;
When he starts that organ singing,
    You got to lay your burden down.

I have often sat and listened,
    As he played along the keys,
At the music softly sighing,
    Like a gentle summer breeze.

Made you think about the angels,
    With their golden harps and wings;
And the mighty songs of Zion,
    That the Christian people sing.

There is music in that organ!
    When Brother Lively plays
He sends the keys a-running
    In a dozen different ways.

## Thoughts of Idle Hours

Then he'd strike the chords so gently,
  In a kind o' solemn way;
And play the sweetest music,
  As the people bowed to pray.

Thoughts of Idle Hours

# BESSIE.

Gentle in nature, modest and shy,
With a sparkle of hope in her pretty bright eyes.
Hope was the anchor she carried each day,
With courage and vigor she made her own way.
Her duties were many, to all she was true,
A dear, loving mother, with bright daughters two.

Thoughts of Idle Hours.

## "A YOKE OF OPPRESSION."

We have been free, yes, fifty years!
From shackles and chains,
But not from tears,
The bloodhound has gone from the cabin door,
The slave master haunts our steps no more;
But a yoke of oppression we sometimes feel,
A yoke that oppresses our common weal.

We've obeyed our rulers,
We've fought for our land;
We've planted the vineyards,
We've gone at command.
But a yoke of oppression we yet still feel,
A yoke that oppresses our common weal.

Be not discouraged, go on to the end;
Be brave men of valor, be women and men,
And the yoke of oppression that is weighing us down,
Some day, like a boomerang,
May turn and rebound.

Thoughts of Idle Hours

# JACK AND I.

Jack and I went out for a walk,
Along the seashore for a pleasant talk,
As we sat on the sand,
By the sad, sad sea,
There Jack gave his heart
And his love all to me.

Said he, "Mary, I love you,
I give you my all;"
Said I, "Jack, don't be foolish,
Love rises and falls.
"Like the waves of the sea,
They are never at rest;
It is hard for you, Jack,
To tell who you love best."

"Now, Mary," said Jack,
"If you don't believe me,
I'll throw myself out
In the wild raging sea."

"Oh! Jack," said I,
"Don't do that for me,
For how on earth
Could I live in the sea?"

## Thoughts of Idle Hours

# THE LADIES' SEWING BEE.

An invitation come for me
To join the ladies' sewing bee,
Which meets at Kitty Paxtons,
On Thursday next, the message said,
And Sally Simpson there will read
A paper on relaxtion.
That sewing bee may be all right
But it requires the best of sight
To make such little stitches;
The only ones that I could make
Would be perhaps a patch to take
And sew on Dollies breeches.
But then you know I had to go
No way to get around it,
When I got there, well I'll declare
I'll tell you how I found it.
The room was filled with tables small,
And chairs pushed back clear to the wall,
And ladies sitting 'round it.
This sewing bee, well now you see,
Was quite a brand new thing to me;
When I went in a lady said,
"Have you your thimble, needle and thread"
Not yet, said I, I come you see
To join the ladies sewing bee.
Your name, please. "Sue T. Horner."
Well now, please take that seat in the corner.
Well, the way those ladies looked at me

## Thoughts of Idle Hours

I was sorry I joined that sewing bee.
At last I was given an apron to make
While the ladies were discussing the way to make cake;
I tried my best and could not sew,
And had fully made up my mind to go
When Kitty Paxton rose and said,
Now, ladies, we'll have the paper read.
Well, Sally Simpson looked too sweet,
Gowned in white from head to feet;
As she arose she looked at me,
'Twas then a quarter after three.
Now, ladies, she said, before I start
I hope no one here will have to depart.
My paper today is on relaxtion,
Which requires much thought and action.
Now relaxtion is this, don't go to pieces,
If Dinnah falls down and breaks all the dishes;
Don't wind yourself up to the highest pitch
Throw Dinnah and the dishes all down in the ditch,
Then sit back and laugh in serene relaxtion.
Don't give a thought to the scene or the action.
The ladies all voted the paper was good,
And said they would try to obey if they could.
"Ladies," said Kitty, "we've been greatly honored,
We'll have a paper next week by Miss Sue T. Horner."
Speaking of me "who sat in the corner."
The work was all finished Kitty gave them to make
Then the ladies sat down to their tea and cake;
It is nice to go to a sewing bee,
But I doubt again if they ever see me.

Thoughts of Idle Hours

## THOUGHTS.

What kind of thoughts now, do you carry
　In your travels day by day
Are they bright and lofty visions,
　Or neglected, gone astray?

Matters not how great in fancy,
　Or what deeds of skill you've wrought;
Man, though high may be his station,
　Is no better than his thoughts.

Catch your thoughts and hold them tightly,
　Let each one an honor be;
Purge them, scourge them, burnish brightly,
　Then in love set each one free.

## Thoughts of Idle Hours

## "WHEN YOU FEEL A LITTLE BLUE."

When you feel a little blue,
Kinder good for nothing, too,
And you try your best to rouse yourself and can't,

Think about the busy bee,
As he flies from tree to tree,
Then stop and take a lesson from the ant.

At the very peep of day,
They are up and on their way,
Toiling on until the setting of the sun.

When the harvest days are o'er,
And they've gathered in their store,
They can rest because their work has been well done.

Thoughts of Idle Hours

## "THE CHORUS."
### TO ARTHUR E. BIRCHETT.

He had gathered in the singers—
  From the East and from the West,
The very best of singers,
  Who could stand, the hardest test.

The Leader, skilled in music,
  Was a man, who knew a tune,
From the plain old fashioned Jew harp,
  To the humming bird, in June.

He'd got them all together,
  And started them to train
Bass, alto and soprano;
  Then, the high-toned tenors came.

"Everybody" joined the chorus
  When Director Birchett led;
Why, the folks just kept on singing—
  Till they nearly lost their head,

Some of them, had long been singing,
  'Fore the Leader here was born,
Some I guess, will keep on singing—
  Until Gabriel blows the horn.

The Leader, mounted high the stand,
  And calmly stood and looked;
Order! said he; the chorus now
  Please take your singing books!

## THOUGHTS OF IDLE HOURS

And turn to No. Thirty Three!
   The "Singers keep their eyes on me.
The bass, will start, right over here;
   Now! Sing your words, with ease, and clear

The Lead Bass, he had lost his place
   Was singing way behind,
Alto and Tenor, stopped at once—
   Sopranos kept on trying.

The Leader. beat and banged! his stick,
   Sopranos, now were flying!
The Lead Bass could not find his place,
   There was no use in trying,

At last the Leader got their ear
   Their hearts were trembling now, with **fear,**
He looked them squarely in the face,
   Said he: Such stuff is 'er real disgrace.

Then, all at once, that mighty chorus!
   Sang out, as if the Heavenly Host"
Had struck their harps' of gold,
   The music! Oh! 'twas sweet to hear,
It seemed to bring Salvation" near
   As on and on, it rolled!

The Leader stood with smiling face;
   Pleased it seemed, was plain,
For weeks and months, he'd labored hard,
   His work was not in vain.

Thoughts of Idle Hours

## "EZIKEL'S FIRST DEGREE"

Ezikel Jones was on the list,
   To take the first degree,
On Friday next the message ran,
   A quarter after three.

Poor Ziek he could not sleep that night,
   No! not to save his soul,
He dreamed he saw a billy goat—
   And climbed a greasy pole.

The appointed day Ziek got there late,
   A quarter after four,
He heard the balls arolling loud,
   Upon the second floor.

Ezikel Jones! was called out loud,
   He answered, "Here am I,"
Please come up front the master said,
   Poor Ziek! made no reply.

You see this pole? Now Brother Jones,
   It's mighty hard to climb,
Take off your coat and necktie too,
   Now start, but take your time.

There is twelve degrees, the master said,
   You'll find them on the pole,
Many a man has gone up there,
   And never had a fall.

## THOUGHTS OF IDLE HOURS

Ziek looked right shy,
   And all at once, he heard a brother call,
The goat is there, Now! Brother Jones,
   To catch you if you fall.

The goat eyed Ziek and Ziek the goat,
   And then he eyed the pole,
How could he climb a greasy pole,
   And never have a fall.

He started up, his foot slipped back,
   The goat was drawing near,
To turn back now would never do,
   His heart was full of fear.

He took one step and slipped back two,
   Poor Ziek was almost crying,
He could not climb that greasy pole,
   There was no use in trying.

So down!. he come right on the goat,
   They round the room went flying,
They caught the goat and found poor Ziek,
   They really thought him dying.

When Ziek revived more dead than live,
   He was a sight to see,
He'd lost his coat and necktie too,
   But had the first degree.

Thoughts of Idle Hours

# HE DIDN'T STOP TO THINK.

Ike Johnson loved a fair young girl,
  Her name was Lucy Prim,
He thought the whole wide world of her,
  And she the same of him.

He took Bill Jones to call one day,
  Which always breaks the link,
He left them there to chat awhile,
  But he didn't stop to think.

Mister Jones he liked the girl,
  And there he told her so,
Just twenty seconds by the watch,
  Before he had to go.

He asked that he might call again,
  Miss Lucy looked at him,
She told him yes and gave a smile,
  Then Ike come walking in.

Jones thanked her and he took his hat,
  And then he went away,
From that time on no thought had Jones,
  But of his wedding day.

Poor Ike his days were numbered,
  Jones did not care a wink,
The trouble about the whole thing was,
  Ike didn't stop to think.

## Thoughts of Idle Hours

## "THE GIRL WHO DOES NOT CARE."

The girl who says she does not care a snap about a man,
   Will do her level best you know,
To catch one if she can.
   Of course she has no time to waste,
On Harry, Tom or Ned,
   Their words were vain,
She had no ear for anything they said.

Such fun you know to come and go,
   And do just as you please,
No one to boss or make you cross,
   One lives in greatest ease.

How years rolled by, she knew not why,
   Her life was sad and lone,
Her friends were few and those untrue,
   She longed to have a home.

Very late in life she became the wife,
   Of a man who lived on a farm,
She had the garden to hoe, and no place to go,
   But to gather the eggs from the barn.

Now girls be wise, "Do you realize,
   How time is slipping away,
When Tom comes round don't turn him down,
   It may be your last chance for a day.

Thoughts of Idle Hours

# "OUR EXPOSITION.

Our Exposition at Richmond, Va., 1915, Colonel Jiles B. Jackson, Promoter.
To Commemorate the Fiftieth Anniversary of Emancipation.

At our coming exposition,
Let us have a disposition
To expose the best we have,
That is good and great to see.

Bring your implements of wonder!
Tear the chain of doubt asunder,
Show the nations our progressions,
Since Lincoln set us free.

At our coming exposition,
Let us have a disposition
To expose the arts and crafts
That are made by you and me.

Bring your trades of skill and labor,
Bring the work of next door neighbor,
Show the nations our progressions.
Since Lincoln set us free.

At our coming exposition
Let us have a disposition
To go up and onward ever,
In the rights of Liberty.

## Thoughts of Idle Hours

He who rules the world and nations,
Truly signed the proclamation,
Show the nations our．progressions,
Since Jesus set us free.

Thoughts of Idle Hours

## "THE OLD-TIME RELIGION."

    Give me dis ole time religion,
    Give me dis ole time religion,
    Give me dis ole time religion,
        It's good enough for me.

Look heah, Brud'er! don't sing dat way.
Dah ain't no ole time religion today;
Dar's a new time kind da's got of late,
A bran new style right up to date.

You go's up now and takes de preacher's han',
And steps right over in de promise lan';
Dar's no use fur to pray, or to speak of a shout,
Fur nobody'll know what you'r' talking about.

Dar's nothing fur to do but to set right down,
Put on your robe and try on your crown;
Den wait fur de chariot to de golden shore;
No use fur to moan and pray no more.

Dar now! Brud'er, I'm sorry fur to say,
Dar ain't no ole time religion today.

Thoughts of Idle Hours

## "DEACON JONES."

Deacon Jones was a real good man,
    As deacons ought to be;
He had one wife, as the Scripture says.
    Instead of having three.

He taught a class in Sunday school,
    With vigor, might and force;
He said no drunkard in the church
    Could join the heavenly host.

Across the way sat Deacon Dodd,
    His face all in a frown;
And tried his best to read so loud,
    The deacon's words he'd drown.

"Not a drop," said Deacon Jones,
    "A Christian ought to take;
No matter what your troubles are,
    Not for his stomach's sake"

Deacon Dodd, he saw no harm,
    In just a sip or two;
If water 'round was hard to find,
    To quench the thirst 'twould do.

When Deacon Jones went home from church,
    His heart was clear and clean;
He'd told them 'bout King Alcohol,
    And pictured well the scene.

## Thoughts of Idle Hours

At night he sought his peaceful bed,
  To rest his weary feet;
Outside the snow was falling fast,
  And turning into sleet.

Next day when he awoke,
  Snow covered all the ground;
And from a cupboard, dark and high,
  He pulled a bottle down.

He opened it, in haste he did.
  And looking quickly 'round,
"I see no harm," said he, "to drink
  When sleet is on the ground."

Thoughts of Idle Hours

## "A FOOLISH MAN."

A foolish man came riding by,
A wise man said, your horse will die.
Said the fool, if he dies,
I'll tan his skin,
And if he lives, I'll ride him again.

Thoughts of Idle Hours

## "SPRING."

Oh! What joy and peace and cheer,
Fill our hearts, when spring is near;
Gone is winter's chilly blast,
Birds and flowers return at last.

Butterflies in dresses gay,
They, too, have started on their way;
Spring is here! Now let us cheer,
The happiest days of all the year.

## Thoughts of Idle Hours

## "LOOKING BACK."

Looking back I see myself,
  A child just five years old;
I'd climb up in my papa's lap,
  When mom began to scold.

He'd hold me on as best he could,
  And then he'd let her fuss;
He did not mind how much she talked,
  Just so she didn't cuss.

And then he'd jump me up and down,
  And tell me 'bout Bo Peep,
Who wandered all around the town,
  And could not find her sheep.

And then he said that poor Jack Spratt,
  He had to eat the lean;
That old Mrs. Spratt, she ate the fat,
  Because she was so mean.

But oh! my mother overheard
  My father tell me that;
From that time on he ate the lean,
  And mother ate the fat.

Thoughts of Idle Hours

## "DOWN IN THE COUNTRY."

Down in the country where we lived,
    The girls and boys were happy;
There was no mamma nor any papa,
    But just plain mam and pappy.

'Twas Uncle Joe and Aunt Maria,
    Uncle Ned and Jerry;
All day long was one sweet song,
    The heart was always merry.

The boys and girls joined in the sport
    Of baseball, kites and marbles;
And when at church the boys sung bass,
    The girls they'd always warble.

Then after school it was the rule
    To see-saw, jump and swing;
The boys spun tops and played hip-hop,
    In fact did everything.

Such happy days and country ways,
    Indeed it was a pleasure;
The greatest joy without alloy,
    And lots of time for leisure.

THOUGHTS OF IDLE HOURS

## "THE WANDERING SHEEP."

Sheep without a shepherd,
   Over the mountains roam,
Weak and worn, bruised and torn,
   Wandering far from home.

Helpless! Shelterless! Wandering!
   "The wolf" can find his prey;
No hand to guide, no place to hide,
   Wandering all the day.

Father, who loves the wandering sheep,
   Bring them into the fold!
They know not, Lord, what snares await,
   Shelter them from the cold.

## "A MAN OF THE HEART."

### To My Friend, Edward Barber.

Give me a man who has a heart,
  To feel another's pain;
Who'll lift a brother from the earth,
  Help him his steps to gain.

Give me a man, who has a heart,
  To bravely stand for right;
When foes assail on every hand,
  Out in the thickest fight.

Give me a man, who has a heart,
  To meet a world of frowns;
With smiling face and courage bright,
  To lift up one who's down.

## Thoughts of Idle Hours

# "AS YOU GO FROM HOME TODAY."

As you go from home today,
Think it out upon the way;
Have you left a kiss for mother,
A loving smile for sister, brother?
Have you bade a kind goodbye,
With your spirit bright and high?
If you have the day is bright,
And the heaviest burden light.

As you go from home today,
Think it out upon the way;
Have you done your very best,
Will your work now stand the test?
Have you conscientious been
In your dealings with all men?
If you have the day is bright,
And the heaviest burden light.

As you go from home today,
Think it out upon the way;
Have you rid your soul of sin?
Are you pure and clean within?
Have you bid the devil go,
Gave him not the slightest show?
If you have the day is bright,
And the heaviest burden light.

THOUGHTS OF IDLE HOURS

## "HE IS RISEN."

Christ our Lord was hung on Calvary,
   For the sins of you and me,
That from sin and condemnation,
   Jew and Gentile should be free.

Jesus Christ our Lord is risen,
   On the third day as he said;
There beside the empty prison,
   Roman soldiers lay as dead.

Early in the dawn of morning,
   "Mary" sought her Lord with tears;
Look! Behold, He is risen!
   See the tomb! He is not here.

He has risen from the prison,
   Bear the tidings far and wide;
Jesus Christ, our Lord, is risen,
   On this glorious Easter tide!

If in Him we die from sin,
   We shall also rise again;
Death no more can have its sway,
   Jesus took the sting away.

## Thoughts of Idle Hours

### TO J. J. PEARCE.

I shall not forget your friendship,
  When the days were dark and drear;
When in trouble, pain and sadness,
  We could find you always near.
I am a prisoner in the darkness,
  Never more may be set free;
But your sympathy, kind and tender,
  Makes the world so bright to me.

As I wait here in the shadow,
  Kindly thoughts shall be of thee;
Praying that the darkness vanish,
  And your pleasant face to see.

Thoughts of Idle Hours

## "NEW STYLE TUNES."
### To Mr. W. H. Marlow.

They've got a lot of new style tunes,
    For old-time hymns today;
Why! you never hear a single hymn
    Sung in the old-time way.

You never hear them singing
    "Am I a soldier of the cross?"
If you did, you'd never know it,
    For the tune has long been lost.

O! I'd love to hear the tunes once more,
    Like mother used to sing;
"And shall I fear to own his cause,
    Or blush to speak his name?"

And then that old familiar hymn,
    "And, am I born to die?"
She'd sing that hymn, so high and sweet,
    'Twould almost reach the sky.

And then she had another song
    About the Judgment day,
"And sinners plunged beneath that flood,
    Washed all their sins away."

These new time tunes may be all right,
    For high-tone folks to sing;
I'd rather hear the old-time tunes,
    Like mother used to sing.

THOUGHTS OF IDLE HOURS

# UNCLE JOSHUA'S BIRTHDAY DINNER.

News had spread throughout the town,
    About a birthday dinner
Uncle Joshua Crow was going to have,
    And invite both saints and sinner.

He didn't exactly know his age,
    He thought 'twas ninety-seven;
He said he'd have one great big time,
    Before he went to heaven.

Uncle Joshua was a kind old man,
    Well-known around the village;
His trade was picking rags and bones,
    And other privileges.

Everybody in the town
    Received an invitation;
And all began at once to make
    Elaborate preparations.

In fact the little town itself
    Was decorated grand;
Ike Simms was there,
    And had on hand his pickaninny band.

The festal day at last arrived,
    It surely was a pity;
To see the folks crowd in that room
    From countryside and city.

Uncle Joshua! greeted them one and all,
  Hypocrites, saints and sinners;
When all had had their turn at him,
  He invited them out to dinner.

## THOUGHTS OF IDLE HOURS

Such shaking hands and bowing down,
   And great congratulations,
Such crowds were never seen before,
   Not in this generation.

Uncle Joshua greeted them, one and all,
   Hypocrites, saints and sinners;
When all had had their turn at him,
   He invited them out to dinner.

The table man! Don't say a word!
   Was loaded down with chicken;
Young spring shote and o'possum, too,
   And lobster still a-kicking.

Cakes and pies, why sakes alive!
   Peanuts, dates and candy;
Blackberry roll and peach preserves,
   Hush! a jug of apple brandy.

Dinner o'er they cleared the floor,
   That music sure was singing;
Miss Dinah Diggs and Uncle Josh
   Come down the floor a-swinging.

He swung Miss Dinah up and down,
   Uncle Joshua's feet were flying;
And then he turned her round and round,
   Miss Dinah was almost crying.

Dinner o'er they cleared the floor,
  That music sure was singing;
Miss Dinnah Diggs and Uncle Josh
  Come down the floor a-swinging.

## THOUGHTS OF IDLE HOURS

The music played, the people swayed,
  Hypocrites, saints and sinners;
'Twas almost day when they went away,
  From Uncle Joshua's birthday dinner.

THOUGHTS OF IDLE HOURS

## "PITY."

Do not stand back and pity me,
If I have fallen in the sea;
If thou hath love, jump in and see,
If you can help to rescue me.

# Thoughts of Idle Hours

## "AS I PASS BY THE WAY."

Keep not your roses,
For my dead, cold clay;
Scatter them along as I pass by the way.

Speak a kind word,
While I'm with you today;
Give me a smile as I pass by the way.

The fairest flower that blooms in the day,
Will avail me but naught,
When I've passed away.

Give me the love that I long for today,
Scatter the flowers
As I pass by the way.

## "TOILING."

Year after year, in toil and pain,
Striving a bit of gold to gain;
Laboring on from day to day,
On earth to live, in stores we lay.

When at last we've gained the gold,
And troubles o'er us no more roll,
Then time steps in and bids us go,
Our days on earth shall be no more.

Others left shall take our place
With braver runners in the race;
Yet toil shall be the lot of man,
It is the Master's great command.

Lay not in store great bags of gold,
But heap up treasures for the soul;
By sweat of brow thy bread shall earn,
Long as the lamp holds out to burn.

THOUGHTS OF IDLE HOURS

## "THE WAR IN EUROPE, 1914."

See the world in great confusion!
   Stop and think oh, mortal man!
Friend and foe alike are losing,
   Thousands fall on every hand.

Why this needless cause of battle?
   Who can answer? No, not one;
Nations, like dumb driven cattle,
   Fall as grass before the sun.

Oh! the world so vast and fruitful
   Why not here content abide?
He who owns the lands and waters,
   Will from us no good thing hide.

## Thoughts of Idle Hours.

## "O, MIGHTY SEA!"

O, Mighty Sea! Thy mournful sound,
  Forever I can hear;
O, tell me what thy troubles are,
  What burdens doth thou bear?

Forever hath thou mournful been,
  What sorrows fill thy breast?
Thy tossing billows never cease;
  Hath thou no time for rest?

Perhaps a message now you bring,
  Up from the mighty deep;
Of loved ones, near and dear to us,
  In watery graves they sleep.

O, restless sea, now pray tell me,
  What message do I hear?
I'll wait beside thy mighty waves,
  And will thy tidings bear.

## Thoughts of Idle Hours

## "THE THOUGHTS OF MAN."

The thoughts of man are seed of nature,
  They grow as wheat, for good or ill;
In planting thought take care to scatter
  Seed of love in deep good-will.

Then watch it grow each day and hour,
  Kissed by the sunshine of the soul;
The seed you've sown will grow in power,
  The fruit it bears will ne'er grow old.

Thoughts of Idle Hours

## "THE BEAUTIFUL WORLD."

The beautiful world, the grass, the trees,
The sweet smelling rose,
The gentle breeze.

The fish of the sea, the birds of the air,
The little tom-tit and the grizzly bear,
Each in its class is a beauty, you see,
In this grand old world for you and me.

The beautiful world, the ice and snow,
The silvery lakes where the rivulets flow;
The rocks and caves, the shells of the sea,
In this grand old world for you and me.

The beautiful world, the mountains and hills,
The wide spreading plains, the valleys and rills,
The beast of the field, the fowl of the air,
In the world there is beauty everywhere.

# Thoughts of Idle Hours

## "CLIMBING UP."

Do not climb so fast, my brother,
   Take your time and go it slow;
Stop and meditate a little,
   Stop and think before you go.

Then when starting do not hurry,
   Take it slowly as you climb;
Stop awhile and rest a little,
   Start again but take your time.

When at last you've reached the summit,
   You will have no vain regrets;
For you've measured well the journey,
   And each difficulty met.
      Take it slow.

## "STOP AND THINK."

Just stop and think a moment,
  When the way seems rough and steep;
When trials, pain and sadness,
  Fill your soul with sorrows deep.

When the mighty waves of trouble,
  O'er you like the billows roll;
Turn your lamp up bright, my brother,
  Take a look into your soul.

# Thoughts of Idle Hours

## "WAITING IN THE SHADOW."

I am waiting in the shadow,
   For the coming of the light,
Bright and cheerful, I am waiting.
   Fearing not the darkest night.

Oh, what peace and consolation,
   As I wait here by the way!
Thinking of the joys awaiting,
   When the mist has rolled away.

Oh, the hand that leads and guides me!
   Sure will help me all the way,
Through the daylight and the darkness,
   While I wait here by the way.

CPSIA information can be obtained
at www.ICGtesting.com
Printed in the USA
BVHW062002290321
603654BV00003B/305